Countdown
to
Valentine's
Day

ISBN 978-0-545-33178-4

12 11 10 9 8 7 6 5 4   17 18 19 20/0

Printed in the U.S.A.   40

First Scholastic printing, January 2011

Countdown
to
Valentine's
Day

By Jodi Huelin

Illustrated by Steve Haskamp

SCHOLASTIC INC.
New York Toronto London Auckland
Sydney Mexico City New Delhi Hong Kong

10 handmade valentines

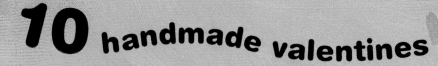

I've made ten special valentines
For all my friends at school.
Each one was made by hand with care,
And turned out really cool!

9 candy hearts

I also have some treats to bring,
Wrapped up in packs of nine.
They're candy hearts with messages
Like "Sweetheart" and "Be mine."

8 chocolates

I've brought a special gift today,
To give to Mrs. Knox.
There is nothing she likes better,
Than eight chocolates in a box.

7 cut-out hearts

To decorate the music room,
We've cut out seven hearts.
Then sprinkled them with some glitter,
For sparkly works of art.

6 valentine charms

My best friend has a gold bracelet.
It holds six pretty charms,
Like hearts and flowers and Cupid,
That dangle from her arm.

5 temporary tattoos

Our class clown Pat has found a way,
To celebrate the day.
With five tattoos stuck everywhere,
All proudly on display.

4-line poem

In class we wrote a valentine.
The four-line type is best.
"Roses are red, " my rhyme began.
I'll bet you know the rest!

Roses are red
Violets are blue
Candy is sweet
and so are you!

3 class moms

The class moms came to school today.
There are three who help our grade.
They brought pink-frosted cupcakes,
And yellow lemonade.

2 heart-shaped cookies

Before I left to catch the bus,
I bought two special treats.
A cookie each for Mom and Dad—
I think they're pretty neat!

1 special kiss

The day just would not be complete
Without one special kiss
From Pop-Pop, who I love so much.
And look! He gave me this!

I'm glad you came along to share
The fun along the way
And all the treats and joy and love—
Happy Valentine's Day!